Table of Contents

W9-DCD-816

Introduction

Zavor is the inspired creation of the minds behind the former top pressure cooker brand in the country. After gaining 25 years of experience in the industry, the Zavor team was ready to set out on their own and is proud to bring you a curated culinary creation for the contemporary home cook. We at Zavor have curated a culinary collection focusing on easy-to-use tools that bring users closer to that healthier lifestyle we all want to achieve. Our unique products offer a simple and healthy approach to cooking that allows users to create a delicious array of meals that are sure to bring family and friends together. From the novice home cook to the expert chef, all walks of life will benefit from Zavor's versatile collection of trustworthy kitchen tools.

Make traditionally fried foods with a fraction of the fat and calories while retaining the color and moisture.

Food is cooked faster, with little to no pre-heating time.

Food is cooked evenly as air circulates all around it.

Air fryers are easy to use and clean.

What is an air fryer?

An air fryer is a countertop appliance that perfectly fries food using very little oil to no oil. Despite the name, an air fryer doesn't actually "fry" your foods. It is essentially a mini convection oven that cooks food by circulating hot air around it. Food is cooked by convection, rather than boiling oil, creating results most comparable to "oven-fried" foods.

Now don't let the name fool you, these machines aren't only for frying. You can also use them to bake, roast, dehydrate, grill, rotisserie, toast, and even reheat foods without having to turn to a microwave.

Why would I want an air fryer?

Air fryers give you that delicious "fried food" feeling without having to actually fry your food in fat or oil. Since you don't need to use oil, the result is a lighter, healthier take on your fried favorites such as Sweet Potato Fries on page 34, Chicken Nuggets on page 68, and Mini Glazed Donuts on page 99.

Since air fryers are much smaller than a typical convection oven, there is little to no preheating needed allowing you to carry on cooking without interruption. Air fryers are perfect for those who regularly enjoy frozen foods, don't like waiting for an oven to preheat, don't cook in large quantities, don't like using microwaves, or are looking for a healthier alternative to deep-frying.

No Oil. No Problem.

Unlike other frying methods (especially deep frying) where oil is needed, the air fryer eliminates this need as it relies exclusively on hot air circulating around food to achieve that crispy, fried feeling. Within a matter of minutes, you can have your favorite foods prepared in a healthier way. Now, that's not to say that you shouldn't or can't use oil, you just have to take it down a notch. If you chose to incorporate oil into your air fryer recipe, do so to the food itself. Do NOT put the oil into the air fryer itself.

Will ALL foods turn out crispy?

Most people often associate "crispy" foods with what we've come to know as that deep fried crispiness. That being the case, the air fryer will not produce the same "crispy" results in all foods. Most vegetables will not have a crispy texture when air fried, but adding bread crumbs will help achieve the crispy crunch we all desire. Additionally, most air fryers come equipped with a timer that will shut the unit off after cooking, significantly reducing the chances of overcooking or burning foods.

Helpful Tips

Where there's smoke... or at least a high smoke point, there's a healthy oil. Should you choose to incorporate oil into your air fryer recipe, the best kinds to use are healthy oils such as safflower oil, light olive oil, peanut oil, and corn oil. The healthiest and most common choice would be light olive oil, so take your recipe one step further and incorporate healthy oils whenever you need to.

A little spray goes a long way. Even though air fryers can cook without oil, giving foods a little spritz of cooking oil spray will help achieve results closer to the deep-fried and breaded deliciousness that traditional frying yields. Give foods a light spray with your preferred oil on all sides before cooking.

Give your food some breathing room. Since an air fryer needs to circulate hot air around all sides of your food, make sure that you do not overcrowd the cooking trays or basket when loading them up. If you need to cook a lot of food in your air fryer, the best practice is to fully cook it in batches first. Then, once your batches are cooked, you can place all the food into the air fryer for 1 or 2 minutes to ensure an even temperature across all batches.

Things You Should Know BEFORE Air Frying

• An air fryer requires proper air circulation, both inside and out, in order to work correctly. Therefore, always remember to keep the vents clear of any obstructions before you start cooking.

• Not all recipes are created equal. An air fryer, while acting similarly to a traditional oven, doesn't necessarily function like one. Recipes for the oven may not always translate to an air fryer oven, so it is important to keep an eye on any recipe you make that doesn't specifically say it is for an air fryer.

• Before placing any food on any of the cooking trays or basket, clean them with soap and water. Whether it's the first time you're using them or if they've been sitting in storage for a while, it's important to clean off any debris or dust that might have accumulated on the air fryer parts.

Let's get cooking!

Not Just for Frying, You Can Also:
- Bake
- Roast
- Dehydrate
- Grill
- Reheat
- And more!

BREAKFAST

Air Fryer Hard "Boiled" Eggs

INGREDIENTS

4 large eggs

DIRECTIONS

1. Place the whole eggs on a tray and place it in the air fryer.
2. Cook at 400°F for 14 minutes.
3. Immediately place the eggs in an ice bath and let them cool completely before handling.
4. Peel the eggs and serve as desired.

Avocado Toast

INGREDIENTS

4 Hard-Boiled Eggs

4 slices whole-wheat bread

2 avocados

Everything Bagel Seasoning Mix:

1 tablespoon poppy seeds

1 tablespoon sesame seeds

1 ½ teaspoons black sesame seeds

1 ½ teaspoons minced dried garlic

1 ½ teaspoons flaked sea salt

¼ teaspoon ground black pepper

DIRECTIONS

1. Place the whole eggs on a tray and place it in the air fryer.
2. Cook at 400°F for 14 minutes.
3. Place the eggs in an ice bath once cooking is complete and let them cool.
4. While the eggs are cooling, toast the bread in the air fryer for 4-6 minutes depending on desired darkness.
5. Peel the eggs once they've cooled enough to handle.
6. Cut the eggs into slices. Mash the avocado to your desired consistency.
7. Spread the avocado onto the toast and place the egg slices on top.
8. Combine all the spices for everything bagel mix and sprinkle as much as needed onto the top.

NOTE If any seasoning mix is left over, you can put it onto a sealable container or freezer bag.

7

Blueberry Muffins

INGREDIENTS

½ cup granulated sugar

½ cup Greek yogurt

½ cup all-purpose flour

1 cup blueberries

1 large egg

½ vanilla bean

1½ teaspoons baking powder

½ teaspoon powdered sugar

Cooking Spray

DIRECTIONS

1. Toss the blueberries in a little bit of flour to coat them. Set aside.
2. Mix the sugar, egg, yogurt, and flour in a bowl. Cut the vanilla bean in half, scrape the seeds from the inside and add into the mixture.
3. Using a hand mixer low-speed, mix for 5 minutes.
4. Add in the baking powder, and then turn up the speed, carefully add in the blueberries.
5. Spray two small 6-well muffin pans with cooking spray. Fill each well 2/3 full.
6. Preheat the air fryer to 325°F for 2 minutes. Then bake each pan separately for 18 minutes.
7. Let the muffins cool and lightly sift powdered sugar over the tops.

NOTE Tossing the blueberries in flour helps keep them from sinking to the bottom of the pan and helps evenly distribute them throughout the muffin.

Breakfast Bake

SERVINGS 8
COOK TIME 1 hour and 13 min

This bake will become a favorite for breakfast, snack, or dinner.

INGREDIENTS

1 (8 oz.) can crescent rolls, refrigerated

1 (12 oz.) package frozen turkey breakfast sausage

1 cup hash brown potatoes, shredded and refrigerated

1 cup cheddar cheese, shredded

¼ cup milk of choice

½ teaspoon salt

¼ teaspoon black pepper

4 large eggs

DIRECTIONS

1. Spray a 9" cake pan with cooking spray and crumble the turkey breakfast sausages into the pan.
2. Place pan on a tray and then on the highest rack position and cook at 400°F for 8 minutes, stirring occasionally.
3. When done, remove pan and drain.
4. Unroll the crescent rolls and press them together to form them similar to pizza dough.
5. When placed in the cake pan, be sure to bring the crescent roll up the sides of the pan. Bake on the lowest rack position at 400°F for 5 minutes.
6. Cover the pastry with sausage, potatoes, and cheese.
7. Combine milk, salt, pepper, and eggs whisking till blended.
8. Carefully pour mixture over the pastry. Sprinkle with Parmesan.
9. Bake on a low rack at 350°F for 30 minutes, covering with foil halfway through to prevent browning the top for too long. Then bake without the foil on at 325°F for 30 minutes.
10. Let it rest for a minute. Serve while still hot.

Cheesy Garlic Biscuits

These biscuits are so wonderful, easy, and addictive!

INGREDIENTS

2 cups biscuit mix

½ cup cheddar cheese, shredded

⅔ cup milk

¼ cup butter, softened or melted

1 teaspoon garlic salt

1 teaspoon dried parsley

DIRECTIONS

1. Mix the biscuit mix, cheese, and milk together until just combined.
2. Place 10 small scoops onto the tray.
3. Place on the middle rack of the air fryer and bake at 375°F for 10-12 minutes.
4. Mix together the remaining ingredients. Reserve ½ of the butter mixture to spread on biscuits when serving.
5. When there are 3 minutes left, brush butter mixture over tops and continue to bake till the biscuits are golden on top.
6. Serve while still hot with the butter spread.

TIP Be careful not to over mix the dough or the biscuits will result in a tough texture.

French Toast Sticks

INGREDIENTS

4 thick slices of challah bread

2 large eggs

1 tablespoon unsalted butter, melted

⅓ cup milk

1½ teaspoons vanilla extract

1 teaspoon of cinnamon

1 teaspoon of powder sugar (optional)

DIRECTIONS

1. Cut the challah bread into sticks about a ½" wide.
2. Mix all the liquids and cinnamon together in a bowl.
3. Spray trays with cooking spray to prevent sticking.
4. Dip the challah sticks in the mixture and then place them on the tray(s).
5. Preheat the air fryer to 380°F for 2 minutes. Add prepared tray once hot.
6. Cook for 6 minutes. Flip sticks and cook for 4 more minutes.
7. Serve while hot.

Optional: sprinkle powdered sugar on the sticks.

Ham, Egg, and Cheese Frittata

INGREDIENTS

¼ cup sliced ham

4 large eggs

½ cup shredded cheese of choice

1 tablespoon red pepper, diced

1 tablespoon green pepper, diced

1½ tablespoons yellow onion, diced

¼ teaspoon smoked paprika

¼ teaspoon ground black pepper

Cooking spray

DIRECTIONS

1. Lightly beat the eggs in a bowl.
2. Slice the ham into bite-sized pieces.
3. Add all the ingredients into a medium bowl and mix till incorporated.
4. Spray a round, 9-inch baking pan with cooking spray and pour the egg mixture in.
5. Place the pan onto a tray in the middle rack of the air fryer.
6. Bake at 360°F for 15 minutes. Then lower temperature to 300°F for 10 minutes.
7. Serve while still warm, but let it rest for 2 minutes before cutting into.

Home Fries

INGREDIENTS

2-3 medium russet potatoes, diced

½ small yellow onion, diced

½ small red pepper, diced

2 tablespoon olive oil

½ teaspoon garlic powder

½ teaspoon onion powder

½ teaspoon salt

½ teaspoon smoked paprika

¼ teaspoon ground black pepper

DIRECTIONS

1. Cut the potatoes into medium sized cubes.
2. Dice the onion and the red pepper.
3. Mix the potatoes, onion, red pepper, garlic powder, onion powder, salt, smoked paprika, ground black pepper, and olive oil in a bowl.
4. Toss the ingredients until everything is evenly mixed and seasoned.
5. Spread out the mixture onto two trays.
6. Bake at 400°F for 28 minutes. Switch the tray positions halfway through.
7. Serve while hot.

APPETIZERS & SNACKS

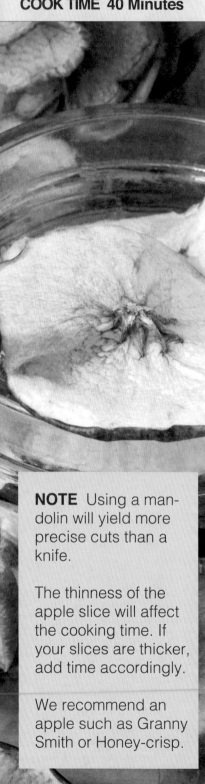

Apple Chips

INGREDIENTS

1 apple of choice

½ teaspoon sugar

¼ teaspoon ground cinnamon

DIRECTIONS

1. Cut the apple into thin slices and remove the seeds.
2. Mix the sugar and ground cinnamon in a bowl.
3. Lay the apple slices on trays with no overlapping.
4. Sprinkle the sugar mix over all the slices evenly.
5. Bake in the air fryer at 300°F for 25-30 minutes.
6. Then crisp each tray individually at 325°F for 5 minutes.
7. Serve once cooled to enjoy a nice crisp chip.
8. Seal leftovers in an airtight container.

NOTE Using a mandolin will yield more precise cuts than a knife.

The thinness of the apple slice will affect the cooking time. If your slices are thicker, add time accordingly.

We recommend an apple such as Granny Smith or Honey-crisp.

Arepas

INGREDIENTS

1¼ cup fine cornmeal

¾ cup all-purpose flour

½ large egg

¼ teaspoon vanilla extract

1½ teaspoons baking powder

¼ cup sugar

1 pinch of salt

1½ teaspoons of cinnamon

2-3 cups of warm water

Optional: 1 cup queso fresco

DIRECTIONS

1. Mix all the dry ingredients and set aside.
2. In a separate bowl, mix the egg with the water.
3. Slowly add the dry mixture to the wet mixture and mix until creamy (sticks a little to the spoon).
4. Scoop with a spoon and form into balls. Place the balls on the trays, leaving space between them.
5. Bake each tray individually at 375°F for 15 minutes on the middle rack. They should be golden.
6. Serve while hot.

NOTE The best result will yield if the trays are cooked one at a time. You can cook the trays at the same time, but you will need to double the time. And at the halfway mark, you must switch the trays positioning with each other.

If you want cheese are pas place queso fresco in the center. Then cover the cheese with the sides, and it should be in the shape of a ball.

Avocado Fries

INGREDIENTS

3 medium-sized avocados

1 teaspoon salt

½ teaspoon cumin

½ teaspoon smoked paprika

½ cup all-purpose flour

¼ cup milk

2 cups of panko bread crumbs

DIRECTIONS

1. Slice the avocados.
2. Put the flour into a bowl.
3. Fill a different bowl with the milk.
4. Combine salt, cumin, and breadcrumbs.
5. Roll the avocado slices in flour.
6. Then dip each one in the milk.
7. Preheat the air fryer to 400°F for 3 minutes.
8. Gently roll the slices in the breadcrumb mixture. Lightly press in the bread crumbs to ensure they stick.
9. Spread evenly on the trays and cook for 16 minutes.
10. Flip the fries at the halfway mark to achieve golden crispy fries.

Basil Pesto Rolls

SERVINGS 10
COOK TIME 10 Minutes

These are the perfect accompaniment to any Italian food!

INGREDIENTS

2 cups dry biscuit mix

2 tablespoons basil pesto, from a jar

¼ cup Parmesan cheese, grated

⅔ cup milk, any kind

¼ unsalted butter, softened

1 teaspoon garlic powder

1 teaspoon dried parsley

DIRECTIONS

1. Mix all ingredients together, except for butter, garlic powder, and parsley.
2. Scoop dough with a spoon and place onto 2 trays. Make sure the dough balls do not touch.
3. Bake at 400°F for 10 minutes.
4. Switch tray positions halfway through.
5. Mix together the remaining ingredients and brush onto tops of rolls.
6. Return to oven and bake a few more minutes till the rolls are golden brown.
7. Serve while still hot.

Cauliflower Crust Pizza

INGREDIENTS

3 cups cauliflower, shredded

1 teaspoon kosher salt

½ teaspoon freshly ground black pepper

¼ cup freshly grated Parmesan cheese

1 cup shredded mozzarella cheese

2 large eggs

1 teaspoon dry oregano

Pepperoni slices as needed

½ teaspoon garlic, minced

½ cup pizza sauce

Cooking spray

DIRECTIONS

1. Shred the cauliflower with a food processor or a box grater.
2. Place the shredded cauliflower in a 9 inch round baking pan and with a fork; toss it a bit, so it is not pressed into the bottom.
3. Preheat the air fryer at 370°F for 2 minutes.
4. Cook for 5 minutes, remove and toss, then place back in for 5 more minutes. Repeat tossing and air frying 5 more minutes, a total of 15 minutes.
5. Pour cooked cauliflower into a tea towel or cheesecloth, twist, and squeeze to squeeze out as much water as possible. Really squeeze hard to get out every last drop.
6. Place cauliflower in a medium bowl along with salt, pepper, Parmesan, 1 ounce of the mozzarella, eggs, and oregano and mix to combine.

7. Take a 1-inch high, 9-inch round baking pan and line with parchment paper, spray with cooking spray.

8. Press the cauliflower mixture into the pan and place it in the air fryer at 400°F for 10 minutes.

9. Lift the pizza shell out by grabbing the parchment edges and then place a new parchment in with more pan spray.

10. Place the pizza shell in and cook again for 10 minutes.

11. Press the crust down more, and repeat step ten.

12. Put the sauce, garlic, remaining mozzarella, and pepperoni on the pizza shell.

13. Place the one in the pan into the air fryer for 4-5 minutes. Remove once browned and melted and lift out pizza by the parchment and place the second pizza in for another 4-5 minutes.

14. Remove, slice, and serve immediately.

Cornbread Muffins

INGREDIENTS

⅓ cup fine yellow cornmeal

⅓ cup all-purpose flour

3 tablespoons granulated sugar

1½ teaspoons baking powder

½ teaspoon salt

⅓ cup milk of choice

1 large egg, beaten

2 tablespoons vegetable oil

DIRECTIONS

1. In a bowl, combine cornmeal, flour, sugar, baking powder, and salt.
2. In a different bowl, combine the milk, egg, and oil.
3. Add the dry mixture to the wet mixture a little at a time until all ingredients are well combined and there are no bits of dry flour.
4. Pour mixture into a greased or nonstick 6-well muffin pan.
5. Fill with the cornmeal mixture about ⅔ full and place the pan on a tray.
6. Bake at 400°F for 20 minutes or until the center comes out clean when poked with a toothpick.

NOTE When mixing the wet and dry ingredients, make sure you DO NOT overmix, so the muffins do not result in a tough texture.

Crispy Bacon-Wrapped Stuffed Dates

SERVINGS 24 Pieces
COOK TIME 14 Minutes

These stuffed dates are enjoyed by everyone! They have a sweet, salty, smooth, and crunchy taste that satisfies every taste bud!

INGREDIENTS

6 bacon slices, cut into 24 pieces

24 smoked almonds (roasted, salted is fine)

24 dates, pitted

½ cup soft goat cheese

24 toothpicks

DIRECTIONS

1. Cut open dates; stuff with ½ teaspoon goat cheese and one almond.
2. Wrap date with a piece of bacon and secure with a toothpick.
3. Lay the date seam down on a tray.
4. Place the tray in the middle of the air fryer.
5. Set to 400°F and cook for 14 minutes.

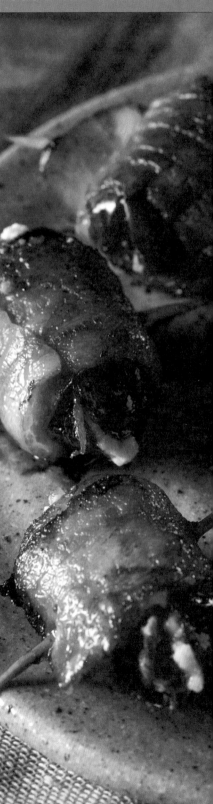

Easy Garlic Knots

INGREDIENTS

1 (7 ounce) package pizza dough

1 tablespoon olive oil

1 tablespoon garlic, minced

2 teaspoons oregano

⅓ cup shredded parmesan cheese

DIRECTIONS

1. Roll out dough to shape into long thin rolls.
2. Shape into knots. Should make 8 knots.
3. Combine the rest of the ingredients in a small bowl and brush them onto the knots with a pastry brush.
4. Place on a tray into the air fryer on a middle rack.
5. Bake at 325°F for 14 minutes.
6. Let them cool down a bit before serving.

NOTE These garlic knots are delicious when dipped in marinara sauce.

Fried Pickles

INGREDIENTS

1 cup whole dill pickles, drained

1 teaspoon salt

¼ teaspoon of paprika or crushed red pepper flakes

¼ teaspoon dried oregano

½ teaspoon garlic powder

½ teaspoon onion powder

2 ounces all-purpose flour

1 large egg

1 tablespoon milk

⅔ cup panko bread crumbs

Ranch dipping sauce as needed (optional)

DIRECTIONS

1. Slice the pickles into chip size pieces.
2. Place the flour into a bowl.
3. Mix the egg and milk in a different bowl.
4. Combine salt, paprika, oregano, garlic powder, onion powder, and breadcrumbs.
5. Roll the pickles in the flour, then dip each one in the egg mixture.
6. Gently roll the slices in the breadcrumb mixture. Lightly press in the bread crumbs to ensure they stick.
7. Heat the air fryer at 375°F for 3 minutes.
8. Spread evenly on two trays and cook for 16 minutes. Place one tray on the second rack and the other tray right underneath.
9. Switch the trays halfway through.
10. The outside should look golden. Serve while still hot with ranch dipping sauce.

Garlic Parmesan French Fries

INGREDIENTS

2 russet potatoes- about 1 pound once cut

¼ cup Parmesan cheese, shredded

1 tablespoon minced garlic

1½ teaspoons olive oil

½ teaspoon salt

½ teaspoon ground black pepper

1½ teaspoons freshly minced parsley (optional)

DIRECTIONS

1. Cut the potatoes into fries. Soak them in cold water for 1 hour.
2. Take them out and pat dry them till there is no residual moisture.
3. Put the cheese, oil, salt, garlic powder, and pepper in a bowl.
4. Gently toss the potatoes in the mixture.
5. Place the potatoes on two trays evenly and then into the air fryer on the second and third rack level.
6. Cook at 400°F for 36 minutes. Switch the trays halfway through.
7. Optional: Sprinkle the fresh parsley on the French fries and serve.

TIPS Soaking the potatoes allows for less starch in the fries and helps them get crispier. You can soak them for 30 minutes if you are short on time.

Make sure to dry the potatoes after soaking. Too much moisture in the potatoes will result in soggy fries.

Kale Chips

INGREDIENTS

1 bag (6-8 ounces) kale leaves

¼ teaspoon garlic powder

¼ teaspoon onion Powder

¼ teaspoon salt

1 tablespoon olive oil

DIRECTIONS

1. Rinse the kale and cut it into 2-inch pieces. Cut off any stems.
2. Pat the kale with a paper towel to get rid of excess moisture.
3. Mix together the oil and the spices in a medium-sized bowl.
4. Lightly brush the mixture evenly on the kale leaves. Try not to have too much oil on the leaves. The kale should be lightly coated.
5. Spread the kale pieces on trays.
6. Cook at 350°F for 7-8 minutes. At the halfway mark, swap the racks positioning.
7. Can add more salt if needed. Serve once cooled.

Onion Rings

INGREDIENTS

1 cup all-purpose flour, divided

1 egg

½ cup buttermilk

1 large sweet yellow onion

2 cups of panko bread crumbs, packed

½ teaspoon salt

¼ teaspoon pepper

1 teaspoon cumin

1 teaspoon garlic powder

1 teaspoon onion powder

Optional: Ranch for dipping sauce

DIRECTIONS

1. Cut the onions into ½ inch thick rings.
2. Place ½ cup of flour in one bowl, set aside.
3. Pour the buttermilk into a medium-size bowl. Then add the other ½ cup of flour and the egg. Mix until well combined and set aside.
4. In a third bowl, combine the bread crumbs and the spices. Mix well.
5. To prepare the onion rings, first coat them in flour from the first bowl.
6. Dip into the wet batter mixture in the second bowl. Let the excess drip off.
7. Roll the rings in the bread crumb mixture in the third bowl till fully coated.
8. Repeat until all the rings have been coated.
9. Spread out the onion rings on the trays.
10. Bake two trays at a time at 400°F for 14 minutes. Swap the trays positioning halfway through.

TIP If you don't have buttermilk on hand, a great substitute is to mix ½ cup milk of choice and ½ tablespoon white vinegar. Pour the vinegar on top of the milk and let it sit for about a minute before using it.

Personal Mini Pizza

INGREDIENTS

1 (7 ounce) package pizza dough

1 tablespoon olive oil

¼ cup of pizza sauce

1 cup shredded mozzarella cheese

1 teaspoon garlic

1 tablespoon oregano

DIRECTIONS

1. Roll out dough to a 9-inch circle.
2. Brush the entire circle with the olive oil.
3. In a bowl, mix the garlic and oregano into the pizza sauce.
4. With a spoon, ladle the sauce mix on the dough and spread with the back of the spoon.
5. Sprinkle the cheese all over the pizza.
6. Place on a tray and bake at 325°F for 24-26 minutes.
7. Remove to a cutting board when done and slice with a pizza wheel to serve.

VARIATIONS
Add ¼ cup of vegetables like mushrooms, pepper, olives, and onions to have a veggie pizza.

Add slices of pepperoni or any other meat like sausage, ham, and chicken as toppings. Make sure the meat is fully cooked before placing on the pizza.

Pita Chips

INGREDIENTS

2 slices of pita bread

2 teaspoons olive oil

1 pinch salt, kosher

1 pinch oregano

1 pinch onion powder

DIRECTIONS

1. Cut each pita slice into as many triangles you would like. Place them on the cooking trays.
2. Mix the remaining ingredients in a bowl.
3. Dip a pastry brush in the bowl and spread onto both sides of the chips; make sure the slices are evenly coated.
4. Cook at 400°F for 8 minutes. Swap tray positions halfway through.
5. Put chips in a bowl, sprinkle with salt and toss. Serve once cooled.

TIP Lightly brush the chips, so there is no excess oil on the chips.

Plantain Chips

INGREDIENTS

2 large green plantains

2 tablespoons olive oil

2 teaspoons salt

2 teaspoons turmeric powder

DIRECTIONS

1. Cut both ends of the plantain and cut slits along the sides of the peel so that it is easier to remove.
2. Once peeled, cut them into thin slices or use a mandolin to have evenly thin slices.
3. In a large container or bowl, add the plantain slices and add enough water to cover all the slices, add in the salt and turmeric powder. Let them soak for 10 minutes.
4. Drain the plantains and pat them dry to remove excess liquid.
5. Lightly brush both sides of the plantain chips with olive oil.
6. Place the plantains on trays. Place one tray on the second rack position from the top. The other tray can be on the second rack position up from the bottom.
7. Cook at 380°F for 20-22 minutes. Swap the tray positions halfway through.
8. When done, remove the chips and serve once cooled.
9. Optional: Sprinkle some salt on top of the chips if needed.

NOTE & TIPS

Cutting slits into the plantain peel is needed because the peel is thicker than a banana.

The time of cooking will depend on the thickness of the chip, so adjust accordingly.

Leaving a green plantain out a couple of days will allow it to turn yellow, which sweetens the plantain for sweet plantain chips.

Potato Chips

INGREDIENTS

1 large russet potato

1 teaspoon salt

1 bowl of water

Cooking spray

DIRECTIONS

1. Cut the potatoes into thin, even slices. You may use a mandolin for more precise cuts.
2. Soak the slices in water for 20 minutes.
3. Spread the slices evenly on the trays. Lightly spray the slices with your choice cooking spray.
4. Sprinkle salt on the slices.
5. Place one tray on the second rack position from the top and the other one right underneath. Bake in the oven at 250°F for 30 minutes.
6. Swap the trays halfway through.
7. After each tray is cooked at 250°F for 30 minutes, cook each tray at 400°F near the top of the air fryer for 5 additional minutes each.
8. Let the chips cool before serving.

TIP If you want to preserve the chips, save them in an airtight container. Otherwise, they will not stay crispy.

Stuffed Pizza Rolls

SERVINGS 8
COOK TIME 10 Minutes

These will become a favorite with kids and adults alike!
Yummy pastry covering seasoned cheese and pepperoni!

INGREDIENTS

1 (8 ounce) can crescent rolls, refrigerated

1 cup mozzarella cheese, sliced

1 teaspoon oregano

½ teaspoon garlic salt

About 24 pepperoni slices

Marinara sauce as needed.

DIRECTIONS

1. Separate the can of rolls into 8 triangles.
2. On the wide end of each triangle place 3 pepperoni slices and evenly spread the mozzarella cheese.
3. Sprinkle with oregano and garlic salt. Roll up, starting with the wide end, folding over ends to seal in the cheese.
4. Place pizza rolls on a tray. Bake at 375°F for 10 minutes, flipping them halfway through.
5. Serve with a marinara sauce for dipping.

NOTE Try not to let the pepperoni and especially the cheese hang off the sides when placing the ingredients on the crescent dough.

Sweet Potato Fries

INGREDIENTS

2 sweet potatoes- about 1 lb.

½ teaspoon salt

½ teaspoon cumin

½ teaspoon smoked paprika

½ teaspoon garlic powder

¼ teaspoon ground black pepper

1 tablespoon extra virgin olive oil

½ tablespoon fresh parsley, minced (optional)

DIRECTIONS

1. Cut the potatoes into fries.
2. Soak the cut potatoes in cold water for 1 hour.
3. Remove from water and pat dry till there is no residual moisture. Too much moisture in the potatoes will result in soggy fries.
4. Mix the salt, smoked paprika, cumin, garlic powder, and pepper in a bowl.
5. Gently toss the potatoes in the seasoning bowl.
6. Evenly spread the potatoes on the trays; brush the tops of the fries with the olive oil.
7. Place the trays in the air fryer on the second and third tray positions and cook at 400°F for 36 minutes. Swap the trays halfway through.
8. When done, remove fries and serve.
9. Optional: Sprinkle the fresh parsley on the fries before serving.

TIP Soaking the potatoes allows for less starch in the fries and helps them get crispier.

You can soak them for 30 minutes if you are short on time.

VEGETABLES

Cauliflower Buffalo Bites

INGREDIENTS

2 cups cauliflower bites sized pieces

½ cup buffalo sauce

2 tablespoons unsalted butter

2 cups panko bread crumbs

½ teaspoon garlic powder

½ teaspoon onion powder

½ teaspoon smoked paprika

½ teaspoon cumin

½ teaspoon salt

¼ teaspoon ground black pepper

DIRECTIONS

1. Fill a bowl with the buffalo sauce and butter, microwave for 40 seconds.
2. Toss the cauliflower pieces in the sauce.
3. Let excess mixture drip off of the bites.
4. Combine the bread crumbs, garlic powder, onion powder, smoked paprika, cumin, salt, and ground black pepper in a bowl and mix thoroughly.
5. Roll the bites in the bread crumb mixture. Make sure to get an even amount on the bites.
6. Place the bites on the trays and cook at 400°F for 30 minutes.
7. Rotate the trays every 10 minutes.
8. Serve while still hot.

NOTE These taste great with ranch or blue cheese dip.

Corn on the Cob

INGREDIENTS

2 ears of corn

1 tablespoon unsalted butter- ½ tablespoon on each ear

½ teaspoon ground black pepper

½ teaspoon salt

DIRECTIONS

1. Set to 400°F preheat 5 mins.
2. Coat the ears with the butter, black pepper, and salt.
3. Place onto a tray and put it into the air fryer on the second rack position from the top.
4. Cook for 14-16 minutes until golden.
5. Serve while still hot.

Crispy Carrot Sticks with Garlic and Onion

INGREDIENTS

1 pound carrots

1 tablespoon olive oil, extra virgin

½ teaspoon salt

½ teaspoon garlic powder

½ teaspoon onion powder

¼ cup yellow onion, chopped

1 teaspoon garlic, minced

DIRECTIONS

1. Cut the carrots into sticks about ¼ inch thick and 2 inches long.
2. In a separate bowl, combine the olive oil, salt, garlic powder, onion powder, chopped yellow onion, and minced garlic.
3. Add the carrots to the bowl and toss to coat.
4. Place the carrots on two trays.
5. Roast them at 375°F for 24 minutes; switch the tray positioning at the 12-minute mark.

TIP To ensure the carrots are evenly coated. Put on gloves or with clean hands, toss the carrots, and the other ingredients in the bowl.

Crispy Garlic Brussel Sprouts

INGREDIENTS

14 ounces Brussel sprouts

1 tablespoon olive oil

1 pinch of salt, kosher

1 teaspoon garlic, minced

2 teaspoons lemon juice, freshly squeezed

DIRECTIONS

1. Cut the Brussel sprouts in half.
2. In a separate medium-sized bowl, combine the olive oil, salt, garlic, and lemon juice.
3. Add the Brussel sprouts to the bowl and toss till evenly coated.
4. Roast them at 350°F for 25 minutes.

Eggplant Parmesan

INGREDIENTS

¾ cup Italian bread crumbs

¼ teaspoon salt

½ teaspoon dried oregano

½ teaspoon garlic powder

½ teaspoon onion powder

¼ teaspoon freshly ground black pepper

¼ cup of all-purpose flour

2 eggs

1 medium eggplant, sliced into ½ inch thick rounds

⅔ cup marinara sauce

1 ½ cups of mozzarella cheese, sliced

1 teaspoon parsley, chopped

DIRECTIONS

1. Combine bread crumbs, Parmesan cheese, Italian seasoning, salt, oregano, garlic powder, onion powder, and black pepper in a shallow bowl.
2. Place the flour in a separate shallow bowl.
3. Crack the eggs into another shallow bowl and beat them.
4. Coat both sides of the sliced eggplant in flour, then in the eggs, and finally coat with the bread crumb mixture.
5. Place the coated eggplants on a plate and let rest for 5 minutes.
6. Preheat an air fryer to 375°F for 4 minutes.
7. Place the breaded eggplants on the trays, making sure they are not touching.

NOTE Best to do the whole breading process in small batches.

8. Cook at 370°F for 14 minutes with the two trays, one in the second rack position and the other in the fourth. Switch the positioning of the trays halfway through.

9. Top each eggplant round with marinara sauce and 1 slice mozzarella cheese.

10. Place the trays back in the air fryer and cook until cheese has started to melt, 1 to 2 minutes.

11. Sprinkle the parsley on top.

12. Serve while hot.

Roasted Asparagus

A classic and easy side dish. Use thicker asparagus stems for this recipe; they are juicier and better for roasting.

INGREDIENTS

1 pound fresh green asparagus
2 tablespoons olive oil
1 tablespoon balsamic vinegar or lemon juice
Parmesan cheese for topping, as needed

DIRECTIONS

1. Break the tough ends off the asparagus spears and peel the bottom third if necessary. The asparagus should be no taller than 7 ½ inches.
2. Pour the olive oil and asparagus in a freezer bag and shake until spears are covered in a thin layer of oil.
3. Place the asparagus spears side by side on a tray.
4. Roast for 14 minutes at 400°F. If your asparagus is very thick, you might need an additional 2-4 minutes.
5. Remove asparagus from the air fryer onto a serving dish, and sprinkle with balsamic vinegar or lemon juice.
6. Top with some parmesan cheese. Serve while still hot.

Roasted Cauliflower

INGREDIENTS

3 cups fresh cauliflower florets

1 tablespoon olive oil

½ teaspoon kosher salt

½ teaspoon onion powder

1 teaspoon minced garlic

DIRECTIONS

1. In a separate medium-sized bowl, combine the olive oil, salt, onion powder, and minced garlic.
2. Add the cauliflower florets to the bowl and toss till evenly coated.
3. Spread across the trays.
4. Roast them at 350°F for 25 minutes. Swap the trays positioning halfway through.

Roasted Cheesy Broccoli

INGREDIENTS

1 pound fresh broccoli

⅓ cup shredded parmesan cheese

1 tablespoon olive oil

½ teaspoon salt

1 teaspoon minced garlic

DIRECTIONS

1. Cut broccoli into medium sized pieces.
2. In a separate bowl, combine the cheese, olive oil, salt, and minced garlic.
3. Add the broccoli to the bowl and toss till evenly coated.
4. Spread across the trays.
5. Roast them at 350°F for 30 minutes. Swap the trays positioning halfway through.

NOTE Instead of Parmesan cheese, use cheddar cheese for a different flavor!

Roasted Green Beans & Onions

SERVINGS 4
COOK TIME 21 Minutes

These green beans take on a completely different taste and texture when roasted!

INGREDIENTS

1 (8 ounce) bag frozen baby green beans, thawed

1 small onion, sliced into thin rings

2 tablespoons olive oil

½ teaspoon kosher salt

¼ teaspoon ground black pepper

½ teaspoon garlic powder

1 tablespoon balsamic vinegar

DIRECTIONS

1. Add thawed green beans and onions to a medium-sized bowl.
2. Toss with all of the remaining ingredients except balsamic vinegar.
3. Place the green beans and onions on trays.
4. Roast at 380°F for 21 minutes or until tender, stirring occasionally.
5. Swap the trays positioning halfway through.
6. When done, remove and sprinkle with vinegar. Serve while still hot.

Roasted Mini Potatoes

INGREDIENTS

1 pound yellow baby potatoes

1 tablespoon olive oil

1 teaspoon kosher salt

½ teaspoon ground black pepper

1 teaspoon fresh parsley, chopped

1 tablespoon parmesan cheese, grated

DIRECTIONS

1. Slice the potatoes in half.
2. In a medium-sized bowl, toss the baby potatoes with the olive oil, salt, and pepper and place on a tray.
3. Place on the second rack from the top.
4. Cook at 375°F for 16-20 minutes.
5. Place the potatoes in a serving dish and top with parsley and the parmesan cheese.

NOTE Parmesan cheese can be substituted with cheddar cheese, and the parsley can be replaced with 2 teaspoons minced cooked bacon.

Roasted Sweet Potatoes With A Kick!

Sweet, caramelized cubes of roasted sweet potatoes with a spicy twist!

INGREDIENTS

1 large or 2 small sweet potatoes

2 tablespoons olive oil

¼ cup dark brown sugar

1 teaspoon cinnamon

½ teaspoon salt

½ teaspoon cayenne

½ teaspoon paprika

1 pinch ground cloves

DIRECTIONS

1. Peel and cube sweet potatoes into ½ inch cubes.
2. Toss the potatoes in a bowl with the remaining ingredients.
3. Evenly spread out the potatoes on a tray.
4. Roast at 380°F for 20 minutes, occasionally stirring to avoid over-browning the tops. When tender, remove, and serve.

Roasted Vegetables

A delicious and slightly sweet vegetable medley that goes well with white meat or it can be served on its own as a light dinner

INGREDIENTS

½ small butternut squash

1 red bell pepper, seeded and chopped

1 sweet potato, peeled

1-2 Yukon Gold potatoes, peeled

½ red onion, chopped

1 tablespoon fresh thyme, chopped

2 tablespoons fresh rosemary, chopped

4 tablespoons olive oil

2 tablespoons balsamic vinegar

Salt and freshly ground black pepper, to taste.

DIRECTIONS

1. Cut the squash, sweet potato, and Yukon Gold potatoes into 1-inch cubes.
2. In a large bowl combine oil, vinegar, thyme, rosemary, salt, and pepper.
3. Add vegetables to the bowl and toss gently.
4. Place the vegetables in a shallow 8-inch square baking dish. Place the dish on a tray and place tray at the bottom position of the air fryer.
5. Roast for 26 minutes at 380°F, or until tender with browning, stir the vegetables gently every 8-10 minutes.
6. Serve while hot.

Santa Fe Veggie Quesadillas

SERVINGS 4
COOK TIME 6 Minutes
per tray

Your family and friends will love these quick, easy, and delicious quesadillas!

INGREDIENTS

4 large flour tortillas

1 packed cup cheddar or Monterey Jack cheese, shredded

½ packed cup whole kernel corn, drained

½ packed cup red bell pepper, diced

½ packed cup black beans drained

2 green onions, chopped

½ teaspoon cumin

½ teaspoon garlic salt

¼ teaspoon black pepper

DIRECTIONS

1. Mix together all the ingredients except for the tortillas.
2. On one half of a tortilla, spoon a generous amount of corn-bean mixture; fold over the other half covering the mixture. Repeat with remaining ingredients.
3. Place the folded quesadillas on the trays making sure not to overlap.
4. Bake each tray one at a time for 6 minutes at 400°F. Flip quesadillas halfway through.

Twice-Baked Potatoes

These are perfect as a side dish and can be made up ahead of time and baked at the last minute.

INGREDIENTS

2 large baking potatoes

2 tablespoons unsalted butter

2 tablespoons cream cheese

¼ cup sour cream

1 cup cheddar cheese, shredded and divided

10 slices of cooked bacon, minced

½ cup evaporated milk

DIRECTIONS

1. Poke holes in potatoes with a fork and place on a tray.
2. Bake for 1 hour at 400°F; turn the potatoes over after 30 minutes.
3. Remove potatoes to a kitchen towel and wrap in the towel until cool enough to handle.
4. Cut potatoes in half and scoop the flesh out into a bowl.
5. Add remaining ingredients into the bowl, leaving some of the cheese and bacon for garnishing.
6. With an electric mixer, beat until smooth.
7. Scoop into potato shells and garnish with cheese and bacon.
8. Place the potatoes back onto the tray in the second rack position from the bottom and bake at 375°F for 10 minutes or until heated all the way through.

Vegetable Kebabs

INGREDIENTS

2 green bell peppers

½ medium yellow onion

½ a zucchini

½ an eggplant

¼ teaspoon salt

¼ teaspoon ground black pepper

2 teaspoons olive oil

18 6-inch skewers

DIRECTIONS

1. If using wooden skewers, soak them in water for 10 minutes before use.
2. Cut all the vegetables into approximately 1-inch pieces.
3. In a small bowl mix together the olive oil, salt, and pepper.
4. Pour the mixture into a freezer bag then add all the vegetables.
5. Toss the vegetables in the bag and let them marinate in the refrigerator for at least 1 hour.
6. On the skewers, add a piece of pepper, onion, zucchini, and eggplant. Repeat on all skewers until they are full but leave a little bit of room on the ends.
7. Preheat the air fryer for 3 minutes at 390°F.
8. Place the skewers on the trays.
9. Put in one tray at a time on the second rack from the top and cook for 12 minutes.
10. Repeat with the second tray.
11. Serve while hot.

TIP You can cook the kebabs with two trays at the same time; you just need to double the time and switch the position of the trays with each other at the halfway mark.

The best result will be to cook each tray individually to ensure even cooking.

FISH & SEAFOOD

Bacon-Wrapped Scallops

INGREDIENTS

16 scallops, cleaned

8 slices of bacon, cut in half to have 16 slices

16 toothpicks

A cooking spray of choice

Freshly ground black pepper (to taste)

DIRECTIONS

1. Preheat the air fryer to 400°F for 2 minutes.
2. Lay the cut bacon strips on 2 trays and put in the air fryer; partially cook for 4 minutes. Switch trays when 2 minutes are left.
3. Once cooking is complete, set the bacon on a paper towel to cool and remove excess grease.
4. Pat the scallops dry with paper towels to remove moisture.
5. Wrap a slice of bacon around the scallop and secure the bacon with a toothpick. Continue this process until there are no more scallops to wrap.
6. Lightly spray the cooking spray over all the scallops and season with black pepper to taste.
7. Arrange the scallops on one tray in the middle rack position.
8. Cook at 400°F for 10 minutes. Flip the scallops halfway mark. The scallops should be tender and opaque, and the bacon cooked all the way through. Serve while hot.

Easy Salmon

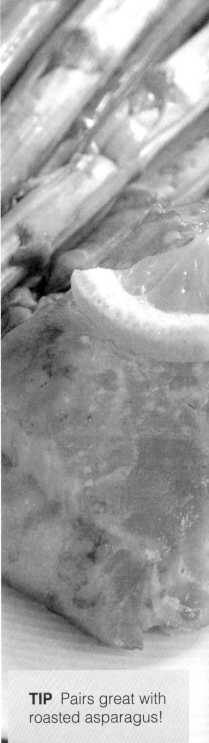

INGREDIENTS

2 6-ounce salmon fillets

1 teaspoon ground black pepper

1 teaspoon salt, kosher

1 tablespoon olive oil

2 slices of lemon

DIRECTIONS

1. In a small bowl, mix together the pepper, salt, and olive oil.
2. Brush the mixture on the side of the fish that is skin-free.
3. Place the fish on the tray with the skin side down.
4. Cook at 390°F for 12 minutes.
5. Serve each fillet with a slice of lemon.

TIP Pairs great with roasted asparagus!

Garlic Parmesan Shrimp

INGREDIENTS

1 (14 ounce) bag uncooked jumbo shrimp, deveined, tails removed, and peeled

1 tablespoon olive oil

1 teaspoon salt, kosher

1 teaspoon ground black pepper, fresh

1 tablespoon lemon juice

4 cloves garlic, minced

2 ounces grated parmesan cheese

2 ounces bread crumbs

1 tablespoon parsley, chopped (optional garnish)

DIRECTIONS

1. Place the shrimp in a large bowl and coat with the olive oil, garlic, and lemon juice.
2. Season with the salt and pepper.
3. Cover the bowl with plastic wrap and let it marinate in the refrigerator for at least 1 hour. It can be in the refrigerator for up to 3 hours.
4. Drain off any excess marinade, so the shrimp is not over-coated.
5. Mix the cheese and bread crumbs in a bowl and toss batches of the marinated shrimp in the bowl. Gently press the breadcrumb mix into the shrimp if needed.
6. Preheat the air fryer for 390°F for 2 minutes. Spread the shrimp on the trays.
7. Cook at 390°F for 12 minutes. Switch tray positioning at the halfway mark.
8. Serve on a plate and garnish with parsley (optional).

TIP The longer you marinate the shrimp, the more lemon flavoring the shrimp will have.

58

Grilled Mahi Mahi with Black Bean Salsa

SERVINGS 4
COOK TIME 12 Minutes

INGREDIENTS

½ cup of soy sauce

½ cup of orange juice

½ cup of ketchup

1 tablespoon honey

Juice and zest of one lime

1 large garlic clove, finely minced

1 teaspoon basil, dried

1 teaspoon oregano, dried

Fresh ground black pepper

4 (8 oz.) Mahi Mahi steaks or fillets, about 1-inch thick

1 tablespoon olive oil, for greasing

SALSA:

2 cups cherry tomatoes, halved

2 large scallions, white and light green parts, thinly sliced

1 (14 oz.) can black beans, drained and rinsed

¼ cup of cilantro, freshly chopped

1 large jalapeño, finely chopped

2 tablespoons lime juice, about 1 lime

Salt and pepper, to taste

DIRECTIONS

1. Place the soy sauce, orange juice, ketchup, honey, lime juice and zest, basil, oregano, and pepper in a freezer bag and mix well.

2. Add the fish fillets and marinate in the refrigerator for 30 – 45 minutes.

3. Toss the tomatoes, scallions, black beans, cilantro, jalapeño, and lime juice in a medium bowl.

4. Add some salt to taste and set aside to let the flavors develop.

5. Lay the fish on a tray and lightly brush with the olive oil and cook at 390°F for 12 minutes.

6. Serve with the black bean salsa and a lime wedge.

Hawaiian Salmon

Marinated in a sweet and spicy marinade and roasted to perfection, you won't believe how easy this is!

INGREDIENTS

¼ cup pineapple juice

2 tablespoons fresh lemon juice

4 6-ounce salmon fillets, skin removed

2 tablespoons brown sugar

1 teaspoon chili powder

2 teaspoons lemon zest

¼ teaspoon ground cumin

½ teaspoon salt

¼ teaspoon cinnamon

4 – 8 slices pineapple rings

DIRECTIONS

1. Combine the pineapple juice and lemon in a freezer bag. Add the salmon filets, seal, and marinate in the refrigerator for 1 hour.
2. Remove the fillets from bag; discard marinade.
3. Combine the brown sugar, chili powder, lemon zest, ground cumin, salt, and cinnamon in a bowl.
4. Rub over the fillets on both sides and both sides of the pineapple.
5. Put the salmon on a tray and add pineapple around it without touching.
6. Place the tray on an upper rack and turn to 400°F; cook for 10 minutes.
7. Turn salmon and pineapple over to let cook for another 4-6 minutes.

TIP If the salmon does not fit on one tray, use two but cook each tray separately to get the best result.

Lemon Pepper Shrimp

INGREDIENTS

1 (14 ounce) bag uncooked shrimp, peeled, deveined, and tail removed

1½ teaspoons olive oil

1 lemon, juiced, strained

1 teaspoon lemon pepper

¼ teaspoon smoked paprika

¼ teaspoon garlic powder

Optional- 1 lemon, sliced

DIRECTIONS

1. Combine the olive oil, lemon juice, lemon pepper, smoked paprika, and garlic powder in a large bowl.
2. Add in the shrimp and toss it in the spices till evenly coated.
3. Let it marinate in the refrigerator for at least 1 hour.
4. Preheat the air fryer to 390°F for 3 minutes.
5. Place the shrimp on one tray in the second rack position from the top.
6. Brush excess marinade mix on top of shrimp if needed.
7. Cook at 390°F for 12 minutes.
8. Put the shrimp on a serving dish and garnish with lemon slices (optional).
9. Serve while hot.

Orange Ginger Shrimp

INGREDIENTS

1 (14 ounce) bag uncooked jumbo shrimp, peeled, deveined, and detach the tails

1½ teaspoons minced garlic

½ teaspoon of pepper

½ teaspoon of salt

2 tablespoons orange ginger sauce

DIRECTIONS

1. Peel, devein, and detach the tail from all the shrimp if not already done.
2. Add the remaining ingredients into a bowl and mix thoroughly.
3. Toss the shrimp into the mixture and make sure everything is evenly coated.
4. Place on one tray in the second rack position from the top, and cook at 390°F for 14 minutes.

NOTE This shrimp pairs excellently with white rice.

Parmesan Crusted Salmon

INGREDIENTS

2 6-ounce salmon fillets

¼ cup Parmesan cheese, shredded

1 tablespoon minced garlic

1½ teaspoons olive oil

½ teaspoon salt

½ teaspoon ground black pepper

1 teaspoon freshly minced parsley (optional)

DIRECTIONS

1. In a large bowl, mix the cheese, oil, salt, garlic powder, and pepper.
2. Divide that mixture and gently press it on top of the fillet side that has no skin.
3. Place the fillets on a tray, skin side down. Preheat the air fryer for 390°F for 2 minutes.
4. Cook at 390°F for 12 minutes.
5. Serve on a plate and garnish with parsley (optional).
6. Serve while hot.

POULTRY

Buffalo Wings

INGREDIENTS

1 pound of chicken wings, with skin

⅓ cup buffalo sauce

1 tablespoon butter

DIRECTIONS

1. Melt the butter in the microwave.
2. Combine the butter and buffalo sauce.
3. Place the chicken in a freezer bag. Pour the buffalo sauce mix into the bag.
4. Marinate the chicken in the refrigerator for at least 1 hour.
5. Place the wings on trays and cook at 380°F for 30 minutes.
6. When done, remove and serve.

Cheesy Bacon Tenders

Easy and delicious appetizers that will make any party a hit.

INGREDIENTS

1 pound chicken tenders- about 6 pieces

6 strips of bacon

6 pieces of pepper jack cheese, cubed- about 2 ounces

DIRECTIONS

1. Flatten chicken tenders, place a cube of pepper jack cheese on one end of the chicken, and starting with the end the cheese is on, begin rolling up the chicken.
2. Wrap with bacon; secure with a toothpick.
3. Place chicken on one tray and bake for 21 minutes at 375°F. Flip the pieces when there is 10 minutes left on the timer.

NOTE These are really good with ranch dressing.

Chicken Nuggets

INGREDIENTS

1 pound of boneless, skinless chicken breasts

½ teaspoon salt

¼ teaspoon ground black pepper

1 tablespoon granulated sugar

1 cup panko bread crumbs

2 tablespoons olive oil

2 large eggs

2 tablespoons all-purpose flour

1½ teaspoon onion powder

½ teaspoon garlic powder

¼ teaspoon cumin

DIRECTIONS

1. To make the chicken breasts the same thickness, pound the meat in any uneven areas.
2. Cut the breasts into pieces to achieve a nugget shape.
3. Combine the salt and sugar in a large container with 4 cups of water.
4. Add the chicken and cover with plastic wrap. Let it sit for 15 minutes.
5. Once the time is done, drain out the liquid.
9. Toss the bread crumbs with oil until the crumbs are evenly coated.
10. Heat the crumbs in the microwave for 2 minutes to give it a golden color. Let it cool slightly.
11. Mix together the eggs, flour, onion powder, garlic powder, cumin, salt, and pepper in a shallow bowl.
12. Make sure the chicken has no excess liquid on it; pat dry with paper towels.

68

10. Working in small batches, dip the chicken in the egg mixture, let the excess drip off.

11. Roll the chicken in the bread crumb mixture. Gently press in crumbs to help them stick.

12. Once all the nuggets are assembled. Transfer them to a sheet pan and place in the freezer. Let the nuggets freeze until completely firm. It can take anywhere from 3-4 hours.

13. Cook each tray individually to yield the best results.

14. Place the frozen nuggets on one tray in the second rack position from the top. Cook at 400°F for 14 minutes. Repeat with the second tray.

15. Serve while hot.

NOTES Goes great with ranch, sweet and sour, spicy mayo, and more!

The nuggets can be made ahead of time and left in the freezer until ready to cook.

The 15-minute soaking helps the chicken remain moist.

Herbed Turkey Breast with Vegetables

INGREDIENTS

1 turkey breast (3.5- 4 pounds), boneless, skin-on, excess fat trimmed

2 garlic cloves, minced

2 tablespoons butter, softened

1½ tablespoons fresh flat-leaf parsley, chopped

1½ teaspoons minced fresh sage

1½ teaspoons minced fresh oregano

1½ teaspoons minced fresh rosemary

1½ teaspoons olive oil

½ large onion, cut into eighths

2 medium carrots, halved lengthwise and cut into 1-inch pieces

1 pound assorted small potatoes, quartered

1 tablespoon olive oil

Coarse salt and freshly ground pepper

DIRECTIONS

1. Dry the turkey by patting with paper towels to remove any excess liquid.

2. Mash garlic and ½ teaspoon salt until a paste forms. Transfer to a small bowl and add softened butter and herbs. Season with salt and pepper.

3. Gently separate turkey skin from breast meat, being careful not to tear the skin. Spread herb butter mixture evenly under the skin, then smooth down to remove trapped air. Brush turkey with olive oil and season with salt and pepper.

4. Place all of the vegetables in an 8-inch square baking dish on a tray. Drizzle with extra virgin olive oil, season with salt and pepper, and toss to combine.

5. Place on the bottom rack position and cook at 400°F for 21 minutes. Stir halfway through.

6. Remove the vegetables once nicely roasted and cover with foil to keep warm.

7. Place the breast on a tray and then on the last rack position. Bake for 13 minutes per pound at 400°F. For example, if 3 pounds, then cook for 39 minutes. Halfway through cooking time, turn the turkey breast over.

8. Continue to bake until the juices run clear when you insert a skewer into the base of the breast.

9. Place the vegetables back in the air fryer for 5 minutes to reheat.

10. Season with salt and pepper if desired and serve with turkey.

TIP Always make sure the internal temperature is reached for food safety reasons.

If desired, place cooking juices in a saucepan and bring to a boil. Mix 2 teaspoons of cornstarch with 1 tablespoon of water and add to the juices. Stir until thickened and use as a gravy.

Honey BBQ Drumsticks

INGREDIENTS

½ cup honey BBQ sauce

1 pound chicken drumsticks, with skin

1 tablespoon smoked paprika

DIRECTIONS

1. Combine the honey BBQ sauce and the paprika spice.
2. Place the chicken drumsticks in a large freezer bag.
3. Add the sauce mixture and marinate in the refrigerator for at least 1 hour.
4. Place the drumsticks on the trays and cook at 380°F for 30 minutes.
5. Remove and serve when done.

TIP Reserve 2 tablespoons of honey BBQ sauce. When cooking the chicken, with 5 minutes left, take the drumsticks out and brush them with the extra BBQ sauce. Put the drumsticks back in for the remaining time.

Honey-Pecan Crusted Chicken Wings

Better than fried and so much better for you!

INGREDIENTS

½ teaspoon salt

¼ teaspoon black pepper

1 pound chicken tenderloins

¼ cup honey

2 tablespoons Dijon mustard

¾ teaspoon paprika

¼ teaspoon garlic powder

1 cup cornflake crumbs

½ cup pecan pieces, finely chopped

Cooking spray

DIRECTIONS

1. Sprinkle salt and pepper evenly over chicken.
2. Combine honey, mustard, paprika, and garlic powder in a freezer bag and add the chicken tenders, making sure all are covered in sauce.
3. Combine cornflakes and pecans in a shallow dish.
4. Coat each tender in the crumb mixture and put them on a tray.
5. Put the tray in the air fryer at 400°F on the middle rack position. Bake chicken 10 minutes, flip and bake 10 minutes more or until the outside is golden.

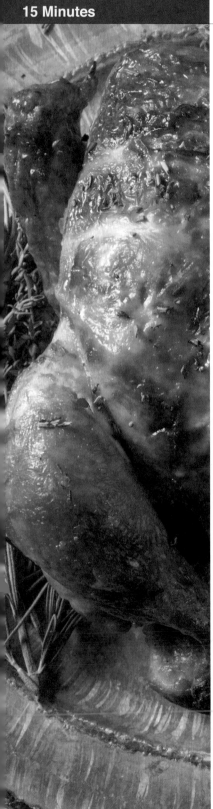

Lemon Herb Rotisserie Chicken

INGREDIENTS

3.5-4 pound whole chicken, or smaller

½ lemon

½ lemon, juiced

1 sprig rosemary

1 sprig thyme

2 teaspoons minced garlic

1 teaspoon dry mustard powder

1 teaspoon fresh rosemary, chopped

1 teaspoon fresh thyme, chopped

1 teaspoon of sea salt

¼ teaspoon ground black pepper

1 tablespoon olive oil

Salt and pepper as needed

Cooking twine

DIRECTIONS

1. Prepare the chicken by removing any contents from its cavity, such as the giblets and patting it dry with a paper towel.
2. Sprinkle salt and pepper inside the cavity of the chicken; then insert rosemary and thyme sprigs. Insert half a lemon. Gently loosen the skin from the breast to place spices on the meat for more flavor.
3. In a small bowl, mix together the garlic, mustard, rosemary, thyme, salt, pepper, oil, and lemon juice to make a paste.
4. Spread half of this mixture under the loosened skin and the rest on the chicken.
5. With the chicken on its back, center the twine and truss the chicken.

6. Insert the rotisserie spit into the tail end of the trussed chicken, going through and out of the neck. Push the chicken down and secure the forks into the chicken and onto the spit. Check to make sure the chicken is centered and balanced by suspending it between your palms over a plate.

7. Use the rotisserie retrieval tool to pick up the spit and chicken and place it in the rotisserie support so it will rotate.

8. Cook at 370°F and set it to rotate for 1 hour. When the cooking time is done, set for an additional 15 minutes.

9. Once done using the rotisserie retrieval tool, carefully remove the chicken, place it on a plate and let it rest for a minute.

10. Then remove the spit and forks, garnish with lemon slices and enjoy!

TIP Wear gloves when dealing with raw chicken to have less mess and for food safety.

If you have trouble inserting your chicken into the air fryer, please see the user's manual for step by step instructions.

Savory Herb Rotisserie Chicken

INGREDIENTS

3.5-4 pound whole chicken, or smaller

2 tablespoons of olive oil

2 tablespoons unsalted butter, melted

1½ tablespoons lemon juice

2 teaspoons salt

½ teaspoon freshly ground black pepper

1 teaspoon onion powder

1 teaspoon garlic powder

1 teaspoon cayenne

1 teaspoon cumin

3 sprig rosemary

1 sprig thyme

2 teaspoons garlic, minced

Cooking twine

DIRECTIONS

1. Prepare the chicken by removing any contents from its cavity, such as the giblets and patting it dry with a paper towel.
2. Rub the inside and outside of the chicken with all the spices. Season under the skin for more flavor
3. In a small bowl, mix together the lemon juice, olive oil, and melted butter. Rub all over the chicken and under the skin of the chicken.
4. With the chicken on its back, center the cooking twine and truss the chicken.

TIP If you have trouble inserting your chicken into the air fryer, see the user's manual for step by step instructions.

6. Insert the rotisserie spit into the tail end of the trussed chicken, going through it and out of the neck. Place both rotisserie forks on the spit and slide them into the chicken. Secure the forks to the spit using the screws. Check to make sure the chicken is centered and balanced by suspending it between your palms over a plate.

7. Use the rotisserie retrieval tool to pick up the chicken and place the spit into the rotisserie support.

8. Cook at 370°F and set it to rotate for 1 hour. When the cooking time is done, set for an additional 15 minutes.

9. Once the cooking time is done, use the rotisserie retrieval tool to carefully remove the spit and place the chicken on a plate, let it rest for a minute.

10. Then place on a serving plate and enjoy!

Teriyaki Chicken Kebabs

INGREDIENTS

1 pound boneless skinless chicken breasts

1 red bell pepper, chopped

1 yellow onion, chopped

½ cup teriyaki glaze

1 teaspoon salt

½ teaspoon ground black pepper

½ teaspoon garlic powder

½ teaspoon onion powder

18 6-inch skewers

DIRECTIONS

1. If using wooden skewers, you must soak them in water for 10 minutes before use.
2. Prepare the onion and pepper by chopping them into 1-inch pieces.
3. Cut the chicken into 1-inch cubes.
4. Place all the chicken cubes into a freezer bag with the teriyaki glaze. Marinate in the refrigerator for at least 1 hour.
5. Assemble your kabobs by putting the red pepper, onion, yellow pepper, and chicken on a skewer. Repeat this order until the skewer is full. Repeat with the remaining skewers.
6. Preheat the air fryer at 360°F for 3 minutes.
7. Place the skewers on a tray. Put the tray in the second tray position from the top.
8. Cook for 30 minutes.
9. Serve while hot.

Optional:

Reserve 2 tablespoons of teriyaki glaze. With 5 minutes of cooking left, brush on extra teriyaki glaze and put it back in the air fryer for 3-4 more minutes.

TIP Try to cut the vegetables and chicken around the same size to help cook everything evenly.

The best result will be to cook each tray individually, but you can cook the kabobs with two trays in; you just need to double the time and switch the position of the tray halfway through.

Turkey Burgers

INGREDIENTS

1 pound ground turkey

2 teaspoons Worcestershire sauce

1 teaspoon hot sauce

1 shallot, minced

1 tablespoon fresh thyme, minced

1 tablespoon parsley, minced

1 teaspoon sugar

2 teaspoons salt

½ teaspoon ground black pepper

¼ cup Italian bread crumbs

½ head of Boston lettuce

1 tomato, sliced

8 slices of pickles

4 burger buns

Spicy Mayo Spread:

¼ cup mayonnaise

1-2 tablespoons Sriracha

DIRECTIONS

1. Mix the ground turkey, Worcestershire, hot sauce, shallots, thyme, parsley, sugar, salt, pepper, and bread crumbs in a large bowl with clean hands until combined.
2. Divide the mixture into four patties.
3. Place the burgers on a tray and cook at 375°F for 8 to 10 minutes.
4. Then flip the burger over and cook for about 10 more minutes.
5. Once the burgers are cooked, let them rest to allow the juices to settle.
6. While they rest, combine the mayonnaise and Sriracha in a small bowl and mix till combined.
7. Spread the spicy mayo on the bottom bun. Then add the burger patty, lettuce, pickles, tomato slice, and top bun. Serve immediately.

TIP The best outcome is when you mix the raw meat with your hands while wearing gloves.

A nice touch is toasting the buns in the oven for 4 minutes at 400°F.

MEAT

Baby Back Ribs

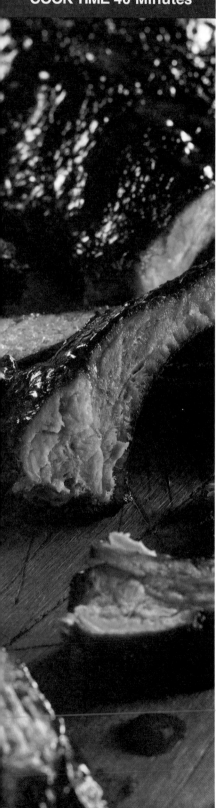

INGREDIENTS

1 rack of baby back ribs- about 2 pounds

1 tablespoon olive oil

BBQ sauce of choice, and as needed

Dry Rub Seasoning:

2 teaspoons salt, kosher

1 teaspoon ground black pepper

1 teaspoon chili powder

1 teaspoon cumin powder

1 teaspoon onion powder

½ teaspoon garlic powder

½ teaspoon dark brown sugar

DIRECTIONS

1. Pat the ribs dry with a paper towel, cut into four sections, and brush olive oil all over.

2. Mix all the ingredients for the dry rub together. Apply all over the ribs.

3. Evenly place the ribs on one tray on the second rack position from the bottom.

4. Cook the ribs in the air fryer at 350°F for 35 minutes. Time does depend on the thickness of the rib.

5. After the 35 minutes, brush the BBQ sauce and cook the ribs for 5 more minutes at 400°F.

Beef Empanadas

INGREDIENTS

1 package of empanada discs

1 teaspoon olive oil, extra virgin

Filling:

1 pound ground beef

1 tablespoon of olive oil

½ medium onion, chopped

1 teaspoon minced garlic

1 cup tomato sauce

1 teaspoon salt

¼ teaspoon ground pepper

½ teaspoon cumin

½ teaspoon onion powder

½ teaspoon garlic powder

½ teaspoon red pepper flakes or hot sauce

¼ teaspoon cinnamon

DIRECTIONS

1. In a hot skillet, add the oil, garlic, and onion. Sauté for a couple of minutes. Add the ground beef and cook till done.
2. Add the tomato sauce, salt, ground pepper, cumin, onion powder, garlic powder, red pepper flakes, and cinnamon to the skillet and mix it together on low heat.
3. Place a little less than ½ cup of filling in each empanada circle.
4. Fold over. Seal with a fork by pressing down to seal the edges.
5. Lightly brush olive oil on the top of each one.
6. Place three empanadas on a tray. Cook each tray separately in the oven at 350°F for 15 minutes. The outside should look golden brown.

VARIATION
Switch the ground beef for ground turkey. Add 2 chopped up hard-boiled eggs for added texture.

Breaded Pork Chops

INGREDIENTS

⅔ cup panko bread crumbs

2 tablespoons unsalted butter, melted

2 large eggs

2 tablespoons Dijon mustard

1 tablespoon all-purpose flour

1½ teaspoons dry mustard powder

½ teaspoon garlic powder

½ teaspoon onion powder

¼ teaspoon salt

¼ teaspoon cayenne

¼ teaspoon cumin

4 (4-ounce) boneless pork chops (about 1½" thick)(1 pound total)

DIRECTIONS

1. Toss the panko bread crumbs with the melted butter until the crumbs are evenly coated.
2. Heat the crumbs in the microwave for 2-3 minutes to give it a golden color. Let it cool a little.
3. Move the crumbs to a medium shallow bowl.
4. Add the egg, Dijon mustard, flour, dry mustard powder, garlic powder, onion powder, salt, cayenne, and cumin together into a medium shallow bowl. Mix till combined.
5. With a paper towel, dry the pork chops to remove any excess moisture.
6. Dip the pork chop in the egg mixture; make sure to let any excess egg drip off.

7. Coat the entire pork chop in the panko bread crumbs. Press the crumbs gently into the pork to help the coating stick.
8. Place the pork chops on a tray and make sure they are evenly spaced apart. The tray should be in the second rack position from the top.
9. Cook at 400°F for 18 -22 minutes. Flip the pork at the halfway mark.
10. Let the pork chop rest for a couple of minutes before serving.
11. Serve while still hot.

SERVINGS 4
COOK TIME 20 Minutes

Cheeseburgers

INGREDIENTS

2 pounds ground beef

1 teaspoon Worcestershire sauce

4 slices cheddar cheese

½ head of Boston lettuce

1 tomato

4 hamburger buns

Burger Seasoning:

¼ teaspoon paprika

½ teaspoon cumin

¼ teaspoon cayenne pepper

1 teaspoon salt

½ teaspoon ground black pepper

½ teaspoon brown sugar

¼ teaspoon garlic powder

¼ teaspoon onion powder

DIRECTIONS

1. Mix the ground beef with Worcestershire sauce and burger seasoning.

2. There should be 4 patties; each one should weigh about 8 ounces.

3. Place the burgers on a tray and cook at 375°F for 8 to 10 minutes.

4. Then flip the burgers over and cook for about 10 more minutes.

5. Top each patty with a slice of cheese.

6. Turn down the temperature to 360°F and cook for an additional minute or until the cheese melts.

7. Once the burgers are cooked, let them rest to allow the juices to settle.

8. Serve on the hamburger buns with lettuce and a slice of tomato.

TIP The best outcome is when you mix the raw meat with your hands while wearing gloves to makes sure all the ingredients are completely combined. A nice touch is toasting the buns in the oven for 4 minutes at 400°F.

Honey Bourbon Pork Tenderloin

So simple, yet delicious enough for a dinner party!

INGREDIENTS

2 pounds pork tenderloin, trimmed

¼ cup honey

¼ cup soy sauce

2 tablespoons bourbon whiskey

DIRECTIONS

1. Trim the pork and sprinkle with olive oil, salt, and pepper.

2. Place pork on tray and place close to the top of the air fryer.

3. Roast at 400°F for 20 minutes on each side.

4. While the pork roasts, combine honey, soy sauce, and whiskey in a small saucepan.

5. Heat over medium heat to blend flavors, lower heat and simmer to thicken.

6. Once the pork is done, let it rest 5-7 minutes and slice into ½ inch slices.

7. Spoon sauce over pork to finish.

Italian Meatloaf with Fresh Basil and Sun-Dried Tomatoes

This tender and juicy meatloaf is a family favorite filled with fresh ingredients and topped with marinara and cheese.

INGREDIENTS

⅓ cup sun-dried tomatoes, packed with oil, drained

½ cup ketchup

1 cup bread crumbs, seasoned

¾ cup yellow onion, finely chopped

¾ cup fresh basil, chopped

½ cup provolone cheese, shredded

2 large egg whites

2 garlic cloves, minced

1 pound ground beef

¾ cup marinara sauce

4 slices provolone cheese, cut into strips

DIRECTIONS

1. Finely chop the sun-dried tomatoes.
2. Combine ketchup, breadcrumbs, onion, basil, shredded provolone cheese, egg whites, garlic, and beef in a large bowl with your hands; we recommend wearing gloves when mixing.
3. Add sun-dried tomatoes to meat mixture and shape into two oval loaves.
4. Place on the tray(s) evenly spaced. Cook at 375°F for 25 minutes.
5. Remove from tray and place on serving dish.
6. Top with marinara and strips of provolone and serve once the cheese is melted.

NOTE To prevent tops from browning too much, cover with foil toward the end of baking.

Mini Italian Style Meatballs

SERVINGS 4
COOK TIME 15 Minutes per tray

INGREDIENTS

½ pound ground beef

¼ pound ground pork

¼ pound ground veal

1 small yellow onion, quartered

2 garlic cloves

¼ cup parsley

1 large egg

⅔ cup Italian bread crumbs (seasoned type)

⅓ cup parmesan cheese, shredded

1½ teaspoon Worcestershire sauce

½ teaspoon salt

¼ teaspoon ground black pepper

1 tablespoon parmesan cheese, shredded

DIRECTIONS

1. Place the onion, garlic, and parsley in a food processor and process till finely chopped.
2. In a small bowl, lightly beat the eggs.
3. In a large bowl, mix the ground meat, onion mixture, eggs, breadcrumbs, ⅓ cup parmesan cheese, Worcestershire sauce, salt, and pepper with your hands; we recommend wearing gloves.
4. Scoop a spoonful of the meat mixture and roll it into a ball roughly the size of a golf ball. Repeat this process until there is no more meat mixture. Yields 12 meatballs.
5. Place the meatballs on a tray making sure you do not let them touch. Cook each tray at 370°F for 12-15 minutes.
6. Sprinkle with remaining parmesan cheese and serve while hot.

TIP If you don't want to cook all the meatballs, you can freeze them. Defrost them when ready to cook and cook at the recommended temperature and time.

DESSERT

Apple Hand Pies

INGREDIENTS

3 tablespoons unsalted butter

4 granny smith apples, cored, peeled, and cubed

½ cup granulated sugar

1 teaspoon ground cinnamon

1 package empanada discs

Sugar Mixture:

½ teaspoon granulated sugar

½ teaspoon ground cinnamon

DIRECTIONS

1. Sauté the butter, apples, granulated sugar, cinnamon, and lemon juice over medium heat. It will take about 15 minutes or till the apples are semi-soft.

2. Put ¼ cup of the filling onto the empanada discs. Brush water around the rim of the discs.

3. Fold over and seal by gently pushing on the edges with a fork. Spray with oil on both sides.

4. Place two to three hand pies on a tray.

5. Mix the ½ teaspoons of cinnamon and sugar. Sprinkle the sugar mixture on the top of each hand pie.

6. Cook each tray separately at 350°F for 15 minutes.

NOTE When sautéing the apples, after cooking, you should be able to cut the apple with a fork.

Brownies

INGREDIENTS

¼ cup cocoa powder

2 large eggs

1 stick unsalted butter

1 tablespoon vanilla extract

½ cup all-purpose flour

1 packed cup dark brown sugar

1 pinch of salt

DIRECTIONS

1. Grease an 8-inch square baking pan that will fit into the air fryer.

2. Melt the butter and stir in the cocoa powder. Let it slightly cool.

3. Whisk in eggs and the vanilla extract.

4. Then stir in the flour, the brown sugar, and the salt.

5. Pour in the baking pan. Bake at 325°F for 38-40 minutes.

6. Let the brownies cool completely before removing from the pan.

TIP The best height for the baking pan is 1.25 inches. It will yield better results if the pan used is not too deep. If it is a deeper baking pan or less than 8 inches, it will need to be cooked longer.

Chocolate Chips Cookies

INGREDIENTS

1⅓ cup all-purpose flour

¼ teaspoon baking soda

½ teaspoon salt

½ cup dark brown sugar

½ stick of unsalted butter, softened

2 tablespoons granulated sugar

1 egg yolk

1 egg

1 teaspoon vanilla extract

1 cup semi-sweet chocolate chips

DIRECTIONS

1. Line tray with foil.
2. In a bowl, whisk together the flour, salt, and baking soda. Set aside.
3. In a separate bowl, combine the butter, brown sugar, and granulated sugar.
4. Add in the yolk, egg, and vanilla extract.
5. Add in the dry mixture, a little at a time.
6. Gently fold in the chocolate chips.
7. Scoop the dough into golf ball-sized balls (about 1 oz). Place on the trays.
8. Preheat the air fryer to 350°F for 3 minutes.
9. Bake for 14 minutes. Switch the trays positioning with each other at the halfway mark.
10. Transfer to a plate or a wire rack to let the cookies cool.

Dehydrated Peaches

INGREDIENTS

2 peaches, peeled and sliced thin.

DIRECTIONS

1. Lay the peach slices on racks.
2. Place the racks in the air fryer and dehydrate for 60 minutes.

NOTE The texture of this will be like fruit leather. If you wish to have it dehydrated more, we suggest adding more cooking time until the desired texture is reached.

Fried Oreos

INGREDIENTS

9 Oreos

¼ cup milk of choice

1 tube of crescent roll dough

Optional: powdered sugar

DIRECTIONS

1. Cut the sheet of dough into 9 pieces.
2. Quickly dip each Oreo into the milk and immediately wrap the whole Oreo in a piece of dough.
3. Preheat the air fryer for 375°F for 2 minutes.
4. Place the Oreos on one tray.
5. After preheating is done, bake for 8 minutes. The exterior of the dough should be golden.
6. Sprinkle with a generous amount of powdered sugar, if desired.
7. Serve while hot.

TIP When dipping the Oreos in the milk, don't leave it in the milk. The Oreo just needs a little bit of moisture from the milk.

Lemon Cheesecake

A light cheesecake, for the perfect ending to a big meal.

INGREDIENTS

1 teaspoon butter, melted

2 ounces graham cracker crumbs

1 to 2 tablespoons of warm water

2 cups of hot water

16 ounces cream cheese, room temperature

3.5 ounces of sugar

2 large eggs

1 tablespoon fresh lemon juice

2 teaspoons lemon zest

½ teaspoon vanilla

5 ounces lemon curd, for garnish

DIRECTIONS

1. Combine crumbs, butter, and the warm water till blended.
2. Spray a 7-inch springform pan with cooking oil and wrap the outside with foil. Pour mixture into the bottom of the prepared pan.
3. Place two cups of hot water in a round, shallow 9-inch pan and then put the pan on the bottom of the air fryer.
4. Place the springform pan on a tray and place above the 9-inch pan. Bake for 10 minutes at 400°F remove from air fryer. When done, remove both pans.
5. In a food processor, place the remaining ingredients except for lemon curd and mix until smooth (there should be no lumps).
6. Pour the mixture into the springform pan over the crumb mixture.
7. Bake the cheesecake at 325°F for 28-30 minutes.
8. Heat the lemon curd in the microwave until softened, about a minute.
9. Spoon out onto cheesecake and spread until smooth.
10. Refrigerate and remove from pan once it has completely cooled.

TIP To check for proper doneness, gently jiggle the cheesecake while still in the pan; the center should giggle more than the rest if properly cooked.

Mini Churros

INGREDIENTS

1 (8-ounce) package of croissant dough

2 tablespoons granulated sugar

1½ teaspoons ground cinnamon

DIRECTIONS

1. Combine the sugar and cinnamon in a bowl.

2. Roll the dough into 1-inch long bite-size pieces.

3. Preheat the air fryer at 375°F for 2 minutes.

4. Place the pieces of dough on the trays and cook for 10 minutes. It should be golden brown.

5. Immediately toss in the cinnamon-sugar mixture. Serve warm.

Mini Glazed Donut

SERVINGS 6
COOK TIME 10 Minutes
per tray

This recipe is great for people who love precise baking and challenge in the kitchen!

INGREDIENTS

¼ cup water
¼ cup milk
¼ cup unsalted butter
½ cup flour
1 tablespoon granulated sugar
½ teaspoon salt
2 whole large eggs, mixed
Icing:
2 tablespoons milk
1¼ cup powdered sugar, sifted
1 tablespoon honey
2 teaspoons vanilla extract

DIRECTIONS

1. In a pot, heat up the water, milk, and butter till it reaches a boil.
2. Turn down the heat and add in the flour. Stir it until it bonds together and forms into a ball of dough.
3. Turn off the stove. Using a hand mixer on low speed, let it run for 1 minute to cool the dough down.
4. Slowly add the mixed eggs in until the dough is smooth and has a shine to it.
5. Prepare a piping bag with a round tip #12 and fill the bag with the dough. If you don't have a piping bag, fill a large freezer bag with the dough and cut off one of the bottom corners to form a ½-inch hole for piping.
6. Put parchment paper on the trays. Pipe the dough into 3-inch diameter rings. The width of the ring should be ½ inch.
7. Bake each tray individually at 370°F for 10 minutes.
8. In a medium-sized bowl, add all the icing ingredients and combine them.
9. Let the donuts cool for 1 minute and then drizzle the icing over all the donuts.
10. Serve while hot.

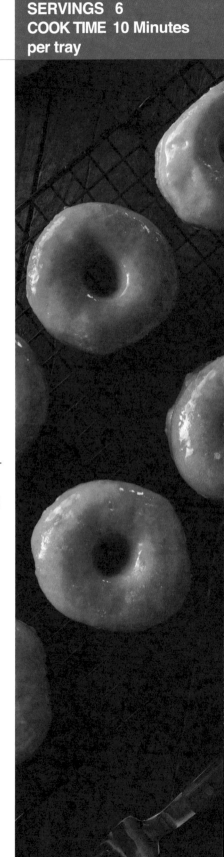

Piña Colada Cheesecake Bars

These luscious bars are delicious but also a nice, light dessert that you will make over and over.

INGREDIENTS

Crust:

1 cup graham cracker crumbs

2 tablespoons flour

2 tablespoons brown sugar

½ teaspoon ground ginger

2 tablespoons butter, melted

1 tablespoon vegetable oil

1 tablespoon water

Cooking spray

Filling:

1 cup cottage cheese

½ cup granulated sugar

¼ cup cream cheese

1½ tablespoons lemon zest

1 tablespoon lemon juice

1 tablespoon pineapple juice

1 dash salt

3 large eggs

Toppings:

1 cup canned cut pineapple, juice drained

¼ cup flaked coconut

DIRECTIONS

1. To prepare crust, combine all crust ingredients in a bowl and mix well.
2. Line an 8-inch square baking pan with foil and spray with cooking spray. Pour crust mixture into the pan.
3. Bake crust for 8-10 minutes at 400°F. Remove and set aside.
4. In a food processor, add the filling ingredients, except for pineapple and coconut, and blend well, scraping sides.
5. Pour filling into pie crust and bake bars at 350°F for 20-22 minutes.
6. Let cool and top with drained pineapple and coconut flakes.
7. When cool, lift the foil out of the pan and cut into 16 squares. Refrigerate.
8. Serve once the bars are completely cool.

TIP For a finer crust, process all the crust ingredients in a food processor in step 1. To check for proper doneness, gently jiggle the cheesecake while still in the pan; the center should giggle more than the rest if properly cooked.

Index